A Child's Life in Korea

by Lucy Ann Sibson
illustrated by Diana Kizlauskas

PEARSON

Scott
Foresman

Editorial Offices: Glenview, Illinois • Parsippany, New Jersey • New York, New York
Sales Offices: Needham, Massachusetts • Duluth, Georgia • Glenview, Illinois
Coppell, Texas • Ontario, California • Mesa, Arizona

Table of Contents

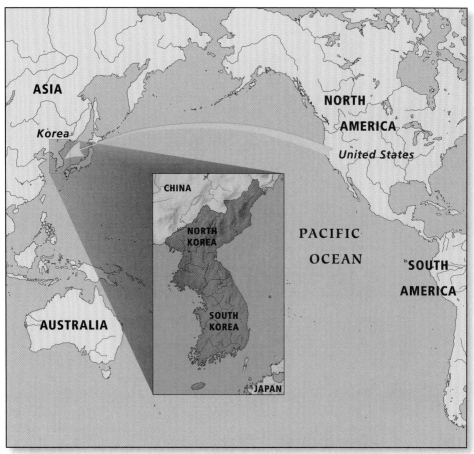

If you travel west from North America, across the Pacific Ocean, you will come to the country of South Korea.

This is Korea

South Korea is a country in Asia. It is far away from the United States. The name *Korea* means "high and beautiful." Korea is high, with many mountains. The capital of Korea is a large city called Seoul.

This is the flag of South Korea.

Korea is a very old country. Its history goes back 5,000 years. But it is also a very modern country. There is a modern airport. There are modern buildings, cars, and factories. In some ways, life in Korea is very much like life in the United States. Children have families, go to school, and celebrate holidays. However, in some ways, life is very different.

School in Korea

Every Monday morning, at every school in South Korea, raindrops or sunshine, there is a morning meeting. First, students gather outside their school. Then, the principal talks to them, to tell them how important it is to do well.

Next, prizes are awarded to students for good work. Finally, children must take off their shoes before entering the school. Why? It is considered rude to wear "outside" shoes when you are inside. At school, each child has a special pair of shoes to wear inside the classroom.

Korean children work hard in school. They study science, language, history and math. Art and music are also very important in Korean schools. Korean children paint at school, but they also go on painting field trips. In music classes, many students take violin lessons. Some take piano lessons. They may also study traditional Korean music.

Family and Traditions

Most Koreans work on Saturday morning, but Saturday afternoon is set aside as family time.

Parents and children might go bicycling or hiking together. They might visit the country. Many people have moved to the city from small farm towns, and they get homesick for green plants and fresh air. Saturday is also a day to visit grandparents. Grandparents are very much respected in Korea.

At home, children do chores and help their parents. They also spend time writing. Korean school children keep diaries or journals. They describe what happens at home and at school. Once a week, they give their diaries to their writing teachers to read.

It is at home that children first learn to leave their "outside shoes" at the door. Children learn to cook their favorite foods. For special holidays, the children dress in traditional Korean clothing, called *hanbok*. At one time, this was how Koreans dressed all the time. Today, hanbok is usually worn only for special occasions. It can bring back memories of the past. Curious children may ask many questions about these traditions.

These children are dressed in traditional Korean clothing.

Holidays in Korea

Solnal and *Chusok* are Korea's two most important holidays. Solnal is the Korean New Year. Families travel to visit relatives. An important part of the holiday is the *sebae,* or showing respect for the oldest family members. Children bow to older family members. This is a serious holiday, and everyone dresses up. But there is also a lot of fun.

    People eat rice cakes and noodles. Traditional games are played, and kites are flown. Koreans have flown kites for Solnal for about 2,000 years! There is an old tale that says that you must stay awake until midnight, to say farewell to the past year, or your eyebrows will turn white. Most children know this is not true, but they like having a reason to stay up late.

Chusok is a two-day harvest festival in the fall. It is often compared with Thanksgiving in the United States. Families get together, and a lot of delicious food is served.

Hangeul Day is on October 9. This holiday celebrates Korean culture, especially Hangeul, Korea's alphabet. People remember King Sejong, who created the alphabet in 1446. There are writing and poetry contests. It is a way for Koreans to remember their culture.